Thought for
the Weak

Preben Andersen

O&U
Onwards & Upwards

Onwards and Upwards Publishers

4 The Old Smithy, London Road, Rockbeare,
EX5 2EA, United Kingdom.

www.onwardsandupwards.org

First edition, published in the United Kingdom by Onwards and Upwards Publishers (2021).

ISBN: 978-1-78815-584-7
Typeface: Sabon LT

Endorsements

Thought for the Weak sums up Preben Andersen. He is thoughtful of all, and especially those who are marginalized and on the edges of society. Each story oozes the 'Great Dane's' consideration of real people, dogs, and the joy of being alive, all etched with his whimsical humour and good cheer. Not the fairy-tales of Hans Christian, but the lived life and faith of Reverend Andersen.

Rev. Gordon Greswell

Having had monthly articles to prepare for a newspaper, I sympathise with Preben's monthly brain-drain to think of something interesting, and something that will keep the reader willing to finish to the bottom of the page. With *Thought for the Weak,* Preben Andersen has managed this beautifully. Woven into his monthly offering, his homespun stories of life, with current affairs, humour and a little bit of religion slipped in, make for an enjoyable and sometimes thought-provoking interval in the day. To include humour in religion of any sort, is an art only practised by a few wise writers. Surely our God or Gods, whoever they may be, must see the funny side of human life, or we would never have the joy of family life, or of companionship or the ability to laugh. I recommend *Thought for the Weak,* not to be read at one 'go', but sipped like a fine wine, enjoyed drop by drop.

Gordon Hill
President
Caldicot & District Branch.
The Royal British Legion

About the Author

The Reverend Preben Andersen is a Methodist minister of religion who, at the age of 70, has recently retired from active ministry to concentrate on his lifelong ambition of writing books. He is of Danish origin but domiciled in Britain since 1977.

He is married to Margaret; they live in Clevedon and have three adult children and numerous grandchildren, many of them living just across from the Severn Bridge. He enjoys writing, reading, walking, Scandinavian crime on TV, and he is hoping soon to join an outdoor bowling club for much needed exercise (says Margaret!)

His writing has proven to appeal to Christians and non-Christians alike and he has written numerous regular articles to the secular press over the years. His aim is always to point people to Christ but in a non-threatening and gentle and often humorous way.

Preben would love to hear from you at any time and has a reputation for replying promptly, so please do not hesitate to e-mail him on *pwandersen@btinternet.com*. This can be for advice, with comments, or to hear more about what he has written over the years in a non-commercial capacity and with any profits mostly going to church charities.

Contents

Introduction

It can be no secret that I have always been a 'scribe' at heart. I just love language and languages, playing with words, translating, interpreting, and in fact it was as a translator and interpreter in Scandinavian languages that I functioned in much of my working life before God called me to the ministry.

Over the years in the *Free Press* newspaper my contributions covered a vast variety of subjects and they were also available on church websites.

So, why did I do this? And why did I not write to the 'already converted' via a Christian magazine instead? Without wanting to sound presumptuous, I always had a lot of time for the great commission in Matthew's Gospel when Jesus says, "Go and make disciples of all nations,"[1] meaning, as I see it, speak (or write) what is on your heart to all (meaning everyone) who are receptive to or in need of hearing (or seeing) God's word.

I was often affirmed in this by people in the street who had the heart to stop and thank me for my column in the paper, and the vast majority of whom we did not see in our churches on a Sunday morning. A lady working at one of the newsagents where I used to pick up the paper even threatened to export me back to Denmark if I dared even think about stopping my column! Honest! Every so often when I felt I might be going a bit 'dry' or running out of 'Thoughts', I wrote to the editor, asking, "Do you really want me to carry on with this?" and every time the answer was, "Yes, we do, your column sits well with our paper." What a privilege that was to hear, and this is the reason why I kept going and reached my 100th 'Thought' before I retired and moved to Clevedon.

Yes, the column is religious but, people tell me, never in an overpowering or 'threatening' kind of way that might be off-putting to those who are still searching. And yes, it contains a lot of humour too. It is sometimes factual and based on world events that happened at the time, but most importantly it is always Bible-based, transcending any particular time and place. And it will never shy away from mentioning the name of Jesus! It is not a blueprint for service preparation, it is not a

---

[1] Matthew 27:19

theologian's paradise, but it is an honest word from a Christian man thanking God for the gift of writing and above all for feeling called to write to His honour in a secular paper.

This was how *Thought for the Weak* started and it ran monthly for the best part of ten years during my time in South Wales. What you now have in your hand is a collection of *The Best Of...* and I wish you happy reading as I pray you may come to know God even better.

So Much To Do!

I tend to write down everything I want to remember. That way, instead of spending a lot of time trying to remember what it is I wrote down, I now spend the time looking for the slip of paper I wrote it on. Sound familiar?

It is a bit like this one, overheard in a conversation between a husband and wife: "I know you believe you understand what you think I said, but I am not sure you realise that what you heard is not what I meant."

We live in confusing times with very many demands on our time and energy. Almost daily, we are bombarded with things to do and to remember. And just sometimes we feel like shouting to God, "Stop the world. I want to get off."

Peace and quiet are precious commodities today which can be difficult to find. However, there is one place where the opportunity still exists: your local church. Yes, gone are the days – sadly – when we could leave our churches and chapels open 24 hours unsupervised, knowing that people would respect them and feel free to enter and leave, to kneel and pray, or just be quiet. And yet, in many towns and villages round the country, the door is open and there is this opportunity – and thank God for it. May we all learn to make more time for those precious moments with God. He knows we need them.

Said the sightseer to the attendant at Beachy Head in East Sussex, "This cliff is dangerous! There ought to be a warning notice." "There used to be," replied the attendant, "but no one had an accident, so we took it down."

Pop into your church and be assured of a friendly welcome or a bit of peace and quiet. There is no risk and the benefit is beyond measure.

October 2011

Lego Nostalgia

I was born in Denmark in the year when LEGO was first produced, namely in the town of Billund in 1950, and they still have their factory there and of course the biggest and original LEGOLAND park.

I guess many of you have visited a LEGOLAND park (perhaps even the Danish one?) and probably (like me) have gazed in amazement at the multicoloured constructions which hundreds of employees spent years creating with literally millions and millions of bricks.

It was not always like that. Back in Denmark, in 1950, the first LEGO bricks were little more than oblong pieces of light brown wood, which you matched with other similar pieces to build a tower, or a house, or something else as long as it was fairly simple. Things were simple in those days.

Now look at it! The sky is the limit! Today's LEGO moves, makes noises, and has engines and flashing lights. And don't we just love it?

Only, for 'oldies' like me, it's all wrong. Give me back the simple things in life. I remember as a child how often my best present was not so much the gift itself as the box it came in. Ring a bell?

Jesus came to earth in the humblest of circumstances, and it all began with a box – a crib – in a stable. But from this modest 'home' grew love, and hope, and joy. And a real understanding for people such as you and me.

Very little is known or written about Jesus' childhood and adolescence, but I dare say that his favourite toys were the rough old pieces of wood He would find in Joseph's carpenter's shop, and then put together to form a cross. A miniature, perhaps, of the cross on which He knew He would die, for you and for me, in love and concern and compassion. Talk about Thought for the *Weak*...

A sobering thought, I think, as we go about the business of our lives at work and at play.

November 2011

21st Century Commandments

I have in my possession a delightful little book with some of the gems that children and young people come out with from time to time. Mine happens to be in Danish, but what I quote below could be from the mouth of any 'babe' regardless of nationality and background.

A group of eight-year-old schoolchildren were asked to think about commandments for today, but with more than a fleeting glance at the Ten Commandments, of course, and these were just some of the classics they came up with, given in no particular order:

- Be as good as you can be before you go and do whatever you want.
- Listen to what your mother says – and to her tone of voice.
- If someone hits you, simply turn a deaf cheek.
- And finally this one: Give us today our daily rye bread. (Rye bread is a staple diet in my homeland.)

More seriously, perhaps, in 2004/5 ITV commissioned a survey to see what the people of today see as their 'current' Ten Commandments, and I give them in reverse order. Some of the answers may surprise you.

10. Protect your family.
9. Never be violent.
8. Look after the vulnerable.
7. Protect the environment.
6. Protect and nurture your children.
5. Do not steal.
4. Be honest.
3. Do not kill.
2. Take responsibility for your actions.
1. Treat others as you would have them treat you.

I can only speak for myself, but if these are really 'the commandments' that a lot of people in our communities today believe in and obey, then I am sure our Father in Heaven will be more than pleased with us. We live in difficult, even dangerous times, but in most if not all of us there is an inbuilt desire to do good, to care and to love. I believe this is the gift of the spiritual dimension in us with which we are all born, whether we really believe it or not, and I believe this is what keeps us going through the difficulties and so often makes us come out stronger as a result.

January 2012

A Danish Christmas

*I*f on Christmas Eve this year your children suddenly ask you to move the Christmas tree into the middle of the living room and then invite you to take each other by the hand and gently walk round the tree as you sing those wonderful carols, blame me! But if after three quarters of an hour of doing this you begin to feel dizzy, blame yourselves!

What you ought to have done is walk in one direction for so long, then stop briefly, get your breath back, and proceed in the other direction.

In many services and at many public events coming up to Christmas I will have shared with people this ancient and still very much alive Danish tradition of walking round the Christmas Tree on Christmas Eve, holding hands and singing the carols. And doing so, we meditate on the wonderful words of hope and joy in the carols and feel our hearts warmed, remembering the joy and expectation of those shepherds in the fields outside Bethlehem. Words as meaningful for us today as they were when they were first written.

As we walk round the tree, we look at one another through the candles (no electric lights) on the branches at the person opposite, and we see their faces (faces we thought we knew so well) shining in the reflection of the candles in a new way.

We see eyes expressing the wonder of Christmas and we feel the squeeze of our neighbour's hand which says, "Today, despite everything, all is well with the world, because it is Christmas time and we are together, here in the darkness, sharing the Light that never goes out."

Even when things are difficult and life is a struggle, the Light of Christmas, Christ Himself, is forever, and for all.

December 2011

An Honest Prayer

*I*t was a blistering hot day, the house was full of guests and things weren't going too well. Finally, the hostess got everyone seated for dinner and asked her seven-year-old daughter to say grace. "But Mother," said the little girl, "I do not know what to say." "Yes, you do," said her mother. "Just say the last prayer you heard me use." And obediently, the little girl bowed her head and recited somewhat hesitantly, but honestly, "Oh, Lord, *why*, oh *why* did I invite all these people on such a hot day?!"

When we pray, may we always expect the unexpected! And if we are in a group of people, may we try to *join* in our heart and soul with the prayer being uttered by someone else.

The poet Coleridge once said that the act of praying is the very highest energy of which the human mind is capable. And I believe he was right. How often do we not go to someone in difficulty saying, "You know, I had in mind precisely what so-and-so prayed for you just now, only I could not express it so well."

We do not know how those people round the dinner table reacted to the little girl's honest prayer, but I dare say that she in her honesty and simplicity helped break what was probably a very tense and uncomfortable moment up until then. Simply by being so honest. And I believe the initial embarrassment was soon replaced by happy relief and a more relaxed atmosphere altogether.

When we pray for those in need, let us expect the unexpected and let us be honest in our petitions. I am sure God does not mind if we stumble over the words a bit or if the prayer comes hard. He knows how difficult it can be, but He knows also what wonderful things prayer in all its nervous energy and perseverance can achieve. So, when next time you say to someone (as we do), "I have been thinking so much about you," why not replace "thinking about" with "praying for", and just see what difference that makes, to you and to the person you are upholding.

February 2012

Kim Larsen's Legacy

*P*erhaps surprisingly, in view of the generally excellent relations between Britain and Denmark (my homeland), Danish pop music rarely makes it big over here! I wonder why? Must be the accent!

Well, one rock singer did try his luck quite some years back now. Kim Larsen is his name and at the time he came across with his band, Gasolin. I am sure you all remember it well? No? Oh, dear…

Unfortunately, Kim and Co. soon ran out of gas. They gave it up as a bad job and returned home. Great shame, really – Kim is very good. And he did sing in English, of sorts.

In the middle of his career, Kim went through a deep personal crisis in his life. Because of the high life as a rock star, he got heavily into drink and drugs and finally debt – and for a number of years he ended up on a health farm in Sweden to 'dry out'.

But lo and behold, he came away a changed man. And his repertoire now contains songs that have a clearly Christian message, even one or two hymns which many Danes almost reckon could be adopted as a new national anthem.

Kim's transformation is not unique. We can only begin to understand what happened in those years on that farm in Sweden. But one thing I do know: Kim experienced a new realisation of the saving power of God that has stayed with him, and while today he remains one of Denmark's prime rock singers, his material has certainly developed to incorporate his newfound belief.

Let us hope Kim might try it again in Britain one day. He certainly has a story to tell. His backing group is no longer called Gasolin, which may be just as well, as people might associate him with fuel and immediately say they would not be able to afford to go and hear him anyway at the going rates at the pumps! But that's another story.

No matter what life throws at us sometimes, there is always hope, and Kim is a living example of that after more than four decades in the music business, and still going as strong as ever. In fact, *stronger* than ever.

May 2012

God in the Open Spaces

*T*he lady regarded the tramp severely. "Have you ever been offered work?" she asked. "Only once, ma'am," he replied, "but apart from that, people have shown me nothing but kindness!"

Joking apart – and it really is no joke – I feel genuinely sorry for the many who want to work but cannot seem to get a full-time job these days. And this goes for people trained in industry and in farming, where there is often so much work to be done but nowadays little or no reward for the toil.

I often ask myself what the church can offer the unemployed other than prayerful support, and I really do hope that once our local Churches Together café is up and running, there may be space to talk to the volunteers and specialists working there, and opportunities for people to be referred to others who can help as well.

Coming back to farming, my first years of ministry were in North Devon, and I lost count of the times I heard a farmer say to me, "It's right here, deep in the field, that I can feel God's presence nearest to me. As far as I am concerned, my field is my cathedral, and not only on a Sunday."

The Methodist Church for which I am privileged to be a minister was (1) born in song and (2) steeped in open air witness and preaching. While we still sing the good old Wesley hymns as lustily as ever in our churches, the open air witness is much more infrequent now – and what a shame. Because what better way to make known and share the love of God with all than in the open outdoors? See and be seen, hear and be heard – surely this is what effective ministry is about, and a great way to engage with people precisely where they find themselves. Personally, I want to focus more on this and encourage others to do the same. I believe our churches have a real responsibility in what is, after all, a Christian country.

If you agree with me, why not visit a local church; you will hopefully find that we are actually a vibrant and dedicated bunch of very ordinary people with a heart for those in our communities who struggle. We are driven and nurtured by the love and compassion of God in what we do, in who we are, and in what we always strive to become, which are beacons of light in difficult times. We want to walk alongside you, not in an interfering kind of way, but listening and acting as we are guided. Are you, and are we, up for it?

June 2012

Unwholesome Peanuts

I like the story about the pastor who called on one of his elderly parishioners and became quite fascinated by the bowl of shelled peanuts she had on the coffee table. During the conversation, he began nibbling on them and soon enough the bowl was empty. He then apologised to the woman for eating all her peanuts, but she replied, "That's quite okay, Reverend, it's no bother. You see, three weeks ago I had all my teeth pulled out, and since then, I've just been sucking the chocolate off the peanuts and putting them in that bowl!"

I am truly sorry if I have now put you off your breakfast this morning, but joking apart and thinking seriously for a moment, does not this illustration describe how many of us come to, and think about, religion these days – in our pick and mix society which is what we are surrounded by? "Come on, let us just suck off what we need and what may do us some good for now and then put the rest aside – the less palatable parts, as it were – at least until a rainy day."

I am afraid God is not someone we can approach just little bits at a time, if at all, and then put aside. It is certainly my own experience that He expects more than that from us and I believe He deserves our best endeavour, even if there are things about Him we find hard to 'crack' immediately.

I was not born a Christian. In fact, it took me twenty years to even begin the journey properly. And without the help and prayer and practical support of so many, I too would probably only be sucking off the top layer still. However, I can assure you that it is the kernel that matters, the inside, and I encourage you not only to believe it but to try it, taste it, for yourself.

All we need to say for starters is this: "Lord, here I am. Use me." He can and He will. God does not work with empty shells. If not always directly and immediately, then in His time He will work with and for you through those who care for Him already, and who care for you at the same time.

July 2012

Did God Answer the Prayer?

"God answers prayer, but we may sometimes fail to realise that He has done so." This is a quotation from that little red and white gem of a book called the *Catechism* for the people called Methodists, which most of us in my tradition have on a shelf somewhere – just like the Bible – but forget to dust off and read very much.

Why do we sometimes doubt that God answers prayer? Because unless the answer is precisely the one we pray for or expect, we often cannot accept that God may reply differently. And how in all the confusion and humdrum of life can we hear what He says anyway?

A Hindu once praised a boy for saving a girl from drowning. When asked why he himself had not rushed into the water, the Hindu replied, "I could not. I was saying my prayers for her."

Who saved the girl? The boy of action or the man of prayer? Or God in or through one or the other? Or a bit of both? I guess that many in today's society would say that the boy saved the girl by his brave action, and by being in the right place for her at the right time. But where does that leave the Hindu? Many church people would say that had it not been for the Hindu praying, God might not have been able to work so well through the boy. Then again, many of us will probably say that both the boy and the Hindu in unison saved the girl. But what does that say about God?

These are important questions to ask and think about, and I want to leave you with this thought from an essay on prayer I wrote at Wesley College during my ministerial training many years ago, particularly trying to define prayers of intercession, which are prayers for others and for ourselves.

"Intercession is setting ourselves alongside God and against the powers of evil. It is to lift situations up to Him and prevent them from going bad. It is to bring people in line with God. It is being active and being seen to be active in a world where God is already in control and acting through the prayers we bring to Him and the efforts we are prepared to make as a result."

I offer these thoughts to you in moments of weakness, and believe me, I have those too.

October 2012

Easter's Open Door

*E*aster is particularly early this year, and one welcome sign of this most important time for Christians, and indeed of spring drawing closer, has to be the daffodils in bloom. Mind you, with the battering our country has received weatherwise over so many months, am I the only one to wonder whether any daffodil can actually survive? And yet, they do. In fact, on my dog Zoe's and my constitutionals in the park we do not see much sign, if any, of real destruction but rather great evidence of God's creation jumping back greener and stronger for all the rain and wind.

Yes, the wind does cause big branches to come thundering down from some of the trees, but the great bulk remains and new buds continue to spring from it. Thinking about it, this might be a fair illustration of Easter, where, following the hardship, the loneliness and agony of Lent, Easter comes with resurrection to replace death and destruction – now, as it always has done.

Easter is without question the high point of the Christian year with its message of hope and assurance for all. And again this year our Christians Together group, consisting of half a dozen denominations, will be taking it in turns to celebrate Holy Week in our various places of worship. Yes, we belong to different traditions and yes, we have different styles of worship, something we all respect and appreciate, but the Easter Hope is a shared blessing and one in which we unite, gladly and with hearts full of praise and wonder. What can be more moving than the joint Good Friday march of witness and open air service, when we recognise the dying Christ on the cross, but above all remember that soon, very soon, come Easter Day, that ugly cross was empty and the Saviour risen and alive for ever? Waiting to welcome us in.

Little Billy, caught in mischief, was asked by his mother, "How do you expect to get into Heaven?" He thought for a moment and then said, "Well, I'll just run in and out and keep slamming the door until they say, 'For heaven's sake, either come in or stay out.' Then I'll go in!"

Thanks to what happened on that first Easter Day, Heaven's door is always open.

March 2013

God Amongst the Disadvantaged

*H*opefully when you read this, the warmer weather will finally be here... The seasons are certainly not what they used to be, are they? Having just said that, Margaret and I shall be going to one part of the world in early June where we should be 'guaranteed' a fair bit of sunshine, namely Uganda.

Most, if not all, major church denominations give their ministers what is known as a sabbatical every seven years. For three months we are encouraged to recharge and reinvent (!) ourselves through a mixture of quality time with family and friends, meditation and reflection, quiet retreats, and written and practical work on a special project. The theme for my sabbatical is 'God Amongst the Disadvantaged'.

For two weeks Margaret and I will be working with Revelation Life, a charity dedicated to helping people living in the slums achieve a better standard of living. For both of us this means moving out of our comfort zones and it is something that I for one approach with a mixture of anticipation and trepidation.

Yet we know that this is what we need to do, and the sabbatical is the ideal opportunity. We have supported Revelation Life for a number of years now, but this is the first time we have had the opportunity to go and see for ourselves the work going on. We have seen videos by those who have been several times, pictures of smiling faces, young and old, who, despite living in the direst of circumstances, sense the presence of God with them – their God who is not a million light years away but right there with them in the troubles, anxiety and poverty, but above all in the encouragement of those working and giving freely and willingly of their time.

Next month I shall share with you what I am up to in July, something completely different but equally challenging. Until then, may the God of encouragement bless you and encourage you in your times of struggle too.

April 2013

A Change of Plans

What a difference a day makes! Hardly had I shared with you last month about Margaret's and my planned visit to Uganda when, following an appointment at the medical centre, we were warned against going, and primarily because of the risk of yellow fever – especially at our ages! Apparently, once you 'climb over' 60, the risk multiplies by five, and that was a risk we were not prepared to take. Instead, we are going to France to spend time with Prospects – another charity close to our hearts – in a summer camp where much good Christian work is taking place for and with people with learning difficulties. You see, one door may close, but God opens another one – again and again. Then, in early July, I shall spend time in quiet reflection on a small island off Tenby with Brother Titus – a Dutch monk who used to be a racing driver! I cannot wait. And in mid-August several members of the Andersen family will be journeying to Denmark to meet with my family there. I guess the three-month sabbatical will fly, and it is good to have something lined up for each of the months.

During the sabbatical I shall give *Thought for the Weak* – and you – a break! Believe it or not, this is the 20th 'Thought' since I arrived on these shores. Doesn't time fly? But God – and the editor – willing, I shall hope to be back again with new 'Thoughts' come September. Unless by then God has put other thoughts about 'Thoughts' into my head...! Who knows?

Have a great summer. I know that for Margaret and me it will be a really interesting one with lots of variety, including precious quality time together. Remember, as I said before, nothing in life is static; we must be prepared to move as the Spirit moves, and initial disappointments (Uganda) can soon develop into new opportunities (France).

May 2013

Sabbatical Return

*S*o here we are again, suitably refreshed and recharged after three months' sabbatical and with so much to write about over the next few months. However, let me say at the outset that I am delighted to be back, not just with the 'Thought', but also into 'normal' church life again. Three months can seem a very long time to be 'out of it' but sabbaticals are not an option, they are there for a reason.

In addition to precious time with Prospects in France, where Margaret and I worked with and for people with learning difficulties, visits to see old friends in our previous church circuits in North Devon and Buckinghamshire, and of course our summer holiday in Denmark – all things which we were fortunate to be able to enjoy together – I was privileged to take in two retreats for myself and also do some serious (and not so serious) writing. The first week away was at Lee Abbey in North Devon and the second week saw me at Caldey Island off Tenby (and much more about that one next month). These were times of quiet and opportunities for much-needed reflection. And in addition to all this I was able to finalise a poetry collection which hopefully will be ready for publication this autumn, and also Zoe the family dog and I put paws to her second book which is now 80% complete and will be launched at the Christmas Fayre at my church in Caldicot at the end of November.

I shall now need to provide Methodist HQ with just a two-page summary of my sabbatical as soon as possible, which means picking and choosing from 36 closely typewritten journal notes. Not an easy job, for sure, but I want to get it done while all is still fresh in mind. My working title for the thesis was always meant to be 'God Amongst the Disadvantaged'. As we go along, perhaps you will be able to judge for yourself how well I stuck to that theme, or not...

For now, great to be back, and thank you to the editor for assuring me that she thinks my page "sits well" with her paper. It is a true privilege writing to you all, but one that I never take for granted.

September 2013

Caldey Island Calling

A mile and a half wide and two miles long, situated off Tenby and only accessible by the small fishing boats that take around 55,000 tourists across every year from the mainland, and back home again by the end of the day. Unless, like me, you had a sabbatical and could spend a whole week.

Yes, I am talking about Caldey Island, one of Britain's holy islands, and inhabited by a Cistercian order of monks who continue a tradition that started in the sixth century. A tradition of prayer, quiet contemplation, a deep-rooted love for community and the individuals in it, and a welcoming heart for visitors. I know. I got to know them and respect them. And I feel I have returned to 'normality' still very much with the tenderness and loving kindness of the Caldey monks in my heart.

My good friend and colleague from Caldicot parish church, the Rev'd Lyndon Harrison, has not long returned from a trip to the island with some of his flock, and they returned with greetings from Brother Titus, the Guest Master, who became a friend during my stay there. You see, we tend to think, if we are not careful, that it is 'them' and 'us', the monks and us so-called ordinary mortals, but it is not like that, and friendships made in Caldey cross every border.

People like me are not born with a dog collar, nor are monks born to a life of solitude and round the clock prayer. We, they, sense a calling, and that calling can come at any time of our lives and often in the most surprising of circumstances. And we decide to answer that call or ignore it, and perhaps we ask God to come back another day or – better still – find someone else! And believe you me, many of the monks have had to make great sacrifices to answer their calls, and life is not always 'easy' for them even now. (Is it ever?) Still they stuck by their choice, trusting God to guide them and inspire them.

When you visit Caldey Island, you feel God's presence everywhere, regardless of whether you are inside the monastery or out and about walking the island. Every step you take and every breath you breathe are God-filled as a result of centuries of people – and monks – living and worshipping and visiting this holy place. I hope to return soon. And I know that the monks, although they were called for and chose their solitude, will always take an interest in the world outside. And we have a duty to share that world with them as they share their world with us so generously.

October 2013

So Many Questions at Christmas!

Christmas came early to this particular Methodist minister when he was asked to go and talk to Years 3 and 4 at Castle Park primary school about his church, his personal faith journey and the early history of Methodism. Never did 45 minutes pass quite so quickly, and rarely have so many questions remained unanswered. We had to limit questions to one per pupil although one young lad had 33 all of his own before we had barely started! Who says religion is dead and buried amongst the young? Don't you believe it! In the end, each pupil walked away with one of my cards with my e-mail address on it and my promise that I will answer every question sent to me – and I shall. As best I can.

I thank God for the opportunities He gives people like me so often to share and, who knows, in His time to spread the Good News. I do not pretend to have all the answers – far from it – but the privilege of sowing a few seeds is beyond words, beyond description. I loved it at school today!

Soon Margaret and I shall be heading for Denmark. And I shall have promoted and hopefully sold a few of my new books, i.e. *Zoe's Doggy Tales Mark II* and my poetry collection *Travellers All*. Never forget you can reserve your copies by e-mailing me on *pwandersen@btinternet.com*.

This has been another good year, and especially so because of the privilege of still being allowed to write this column despite the three months' sabbatical break when it could so easily have stopped never to resume again. I always thank God for the patience of the editor!

Assuming and hoping that I may be permitted a special word for Christmas in mid-December, I shall refrain from wishing you all a merry Christmas just yet (although I think I just did!) but leave you, as I started, with words of thanks for all the blessings God gives us here in this locality. I really do feel there is a spirit about the place and that Spirit is taking us in all sorts of directions. Castle Park is but one example but such an important one. I wonder if the first question is in my inbox yet? Something did go *pling* just now! And I would not be surprised if some of those questions become subjects for future 'Thoughts'.

December 2013

Shalom Peace

*I*t is a well-known fact, in our churches at least, that the Greeks have not just one but four words for love. But I wonder how well known is the fact that the Hebrews who put together the Old Testament in the Hebrew language had at least one word with probably a couple of dozen meanings, at least? Yes? No? Well, they did, and that word is *Shalom*.

The most common English translation of the word always was – and is – 'Peace'. And there is nothing wrong with that, especially when we remember that *Shalom* was said both as a greeting and when you bid people farewell. *Shalom* – peace be with you. However, we miss some of the point if we leave it at that.

It is now generally agreed that in this one word we have the following sentiments too, all in one form or another connected with peace: contentment, completeness, wholeness, harmony, welfare, fullness and the total absence of agitation or discord. I could go on but might run out of space.

So, when Jesus used this word – *Shalom* – and He often did, I have no doubt that He would wish on his recipient not just one or two but all of those attributes. In fact, I am sure of it. It is a beautiful word and, if said with feeling, can convey so much love and truth. Try it.

One of my Christmas presents from Margaret was Nelson Mandela's autobiography, *Long Walk to Freedom*, on which the cinema film of the same name is based. The book consists of 700 pages but I find it very hard to put down. If ever there was a man in modern times who, like Jesus, knew and tried to live the word *Shalom*, Mandela was one. Just look at those definitions again. However, we should be careful not to turn Mandela into a saint, for by his own admission he did not get everything right and he made many mistakes on his long and often lonesome and frequently dangerous walk. Only one, Jesus, totally human yet totally divine, did ever and will ever exemplify *all* the attributes of the word in action, but that should not stop the rest of us from striving to learn about more of them and live them better.

Dare I say it, just once more? *SHALOM!*

January 2014

Easter Hope

*M*argaret's and my summer holidays this year will be spent in Malta in late June and early July, so we hardly need our coats and woollen scarves for that one! Margaret has family living in Malta so it is always good to go and catch up, and still at the same time be ourselves and do what we want to do without asking anyone's permission first.

Holidays are for relaxing and recharging, and Malta gives the opportunity for all that and much more, although personally I have to say that I much prefer the slower pace of life and greener environment of the sister island Gozo to the rush of the mainland. Just think, four hundred thousand people crowded into a country not much bigger than the Isle of Wight! And that is without counting the tourists.

As I write this, we are coming up to Mothering Sunday, which is always a welcome and pleasant oasis at the time of Lent when, travelling with Jesus through His suffering and temptation, we can sometimes feel a bit despondent about things. However, soon Easter will be here and just at the right time, with the joy of spring and everything else that we know will give us that extra boost and desire to get up and go again. Just like holidays do.

Coming back to Malta, off the mainland we find St Paul's Island, which is little more than a small and very rocky stretch of land where supposedly the great apostle shipwrecked and subsequently converted the whole population to his – or should I say God's – way of thinking. After the pain and the danger of the shipwreck came the hope and the light of the gospel, and I know of few places where that awareness of the presence of God is as evident as in Malta and Gozo. They say there is one church for every day of the year on those islands alone. I have never counted them despite many a visit over the years, but I have no doubt about the statistic.

May the Peace and the Joy and the Hope of Easter be a real blessing to you all as after the pain of Good Friday we arrive at the assurance of Easter Day. There is no greater opportunity for Christians (and for anyone still searching) to seek the Light of Christ and to make it their own.

April 2014

Why I Love Danish Crime Novels

*W*hat do you like reading? Well, I guess there are as many answers to this question as there are people. You will not be surprised to hear that being a Dane, I enjoy a good Scandinavian crime novel in my spare time.

Enjoy? How can you enjoy a good murder, I hear you whisper, and that coming from someone who goes green and blue when other members of the family watch Casualty and Holby City. Well, I guess it has something to do with the atmosphere and settings of Danish and Swedish crime, very black and cruel at times, and yet full of suspense and the magic of nature everywhere.

This reminds me very much of the setting when Jesus was tempted by Satan in the desert, and the latter pointed out and even took Jesus to the temple walls, from where he promised Him the earth, literally, if only He would succumb to the tempter. Thankfully that never happened. From the desert sand to the highest pinnacle, and anywhere in between, Jesus not only held His own but conquered evil, forever and for all. Now, that is worth celebrating!

And however 'bleak' my Danish novels – and honestly, I do *not* preach on them in my sermons, they are for 'leisure' only – this bleakness pales into insignificance when compared to the dangers and the hate and the murderous villains Jesus had to face. The cruelty levelled at Him was unspeakable, and no book can ever begin to match it. Even the Bible avoids all the detail but gives us enough to know the full scale of the atrocities. A bit like TV today, when at least we have a screen between us and the events and yet know very well how gruesome the world can be. At times so cruel that we can forget all that is good and true and beautiful. Yet we must never forget the good inherent in most of us. We should hold on to it and treasure it instead.

Jesus by His example gives us every reason to do just that, and we must.

September 2014

What Can I Give Him, Poor As I Am?

The Ebola virus continues to sweep western African countries and remains a threat to us all if not curtailed or, better still, erased completely. Thousands of people throughout the world try to help in whichever way they can, be it physically by going out to the troubled countries as nurses and doctors to heal and to train people, with little or no regard for their own wellbeing, or financially and prayerfully, which is something we all can and should be doing.

The Methodist Relief & Development Fund charity as was (now renamed All We Can), has on their website a beautiful Ebola prayer, which goes like this (slightly abbreviated): "Lord of all nations, we pray for the people of West Africa. We pray that the Ebola virus is contained and its impact limited. We pray for those who have already been affected, for families grieving for the loss of loved ones, for communities living in fear, and for health workers and local volunteers doing all they can to provide protection, comfort and prevention."

The founder of the Methodist Church, John Wesley (1703-91), had as his motto, "Do all the good you can. By all the means you can. In all the ways you can. In all the places you can. At all the times you can. To all the people you can. As long as ever you can." I, for one, feel privileged to belong to a tradition where this is still very much our aim.

You may now ask, "But what can I give, I who have so little to give and to spare?" I think the answer is in that beautiful Christmas hymn *In the Bleak Midwinter* (my Margaret's favourite), where in the last verse we read and sing this: "What can I give Him, poor as I am? If I were a shepherd, I would bring a lamb; if I were a wise man, I would do my part; yet what I can I give Him – give my heart."

So let us remember the Ebola prayer, for there is no quick-fix solution to this, and let us put our heart, soul and mind into all that we do for our neighbours, wherever and whoever they are. God wants no more from us but expects no less.

November 2014

God-Connections at Christmas

Christmas has certainly arrived early at my church this year. As I am writing this (in late November), MENCAP has started with us on Monday mornings, where for the moment coffee, tea and delicious cakes are being served, with the possibility of light lunches as we/they go along. And only today did I meet with a representative for MOO-MUSIC, which specializes in musical activities for the 0-5 year age group, and they are going to start at our church in January next year.

Neither the MENCAP nor MOO-MUSIC enquiries came about through any intervention by myself or any of my church members; they came as a bolt from the blue, and I am so grateful that I have a church and members who are as keen as I am to open our doors to community organisations so that we can all work together and provide a safe space for meeting together.

We have so much to be grateful for, and we are. And I guess what I am trying to say is that much of what happens in our local community, and indeed in the world at large, often comes unexpectedly and surprisingly, as in these two examples.

Jesus certainly came like a bolt from the blue, to appear first to shepherds outside Bethlehem, and then – much later – to be found in Nazareth by the 'wise men' from the East. God sent Christ to an occupied land, to a people in despair, persecuted and frightened, to offer hope and love and assurance.

We can so easily tend to forget in this day and time the love and the goodness surrounding us. It can get drowned in negativity, anxiety and downright fear. However, Christmas is the time for resounding joy and eternal hope, and for taking the God-given opportunities as they appear to us. We certainly try to do that at Caldicot Methodist Church, and it is my Christmas prayer that in whatever situation you find yourself, you may want and be able to do the same.

You see, although in one way our Saviour came like a bolt from the blue – unexpectedly – He had nevertheless been foretold by the prophets over thousands of years; we were just not ready to believe and welcome Him. So, are we ready now, knowing that one day He will come again?

And are we preparing properly by opening our doors to those in need of, and seeking, a Home?

Happy Christmas!

December 2014

Was God in the Earthquake?

I am sure no heart can have been untouched by the news of the earthquake in Nepal, nor by the immediate support and generosity by the British people through DEC with £19,000,000 raised in just the first 24 hours.

So often when natural disasters like this take place, people will say, "Where is God in all this?" or, "How can God let this happen?" and while this is an understandable and very human reaction, the Old Testament book of Kings has this magnificent passage in chapter 19: "A very strong wind blew until it caused the mountains to fall apart and large rocks to break in front of the Lord. But the Lord was not in the wind. After the wind, there was an earthquake, but the Lord was not in the earthquake. After the earthquake, there was a fire, but the Lord was not in the fire. After the fire, there was a quiet, gentle sound..."

I don't know about you, but that quiet, gentle sound – and voice – of God springs to my mind as, writing this, I hear about a teenage boy salvaged from the ruins in Nepal after five days buried in the rubble, having survived on practically nothing. A miracle indeed, if only one in all the death, pain and desolation of everything else surrounding him. And you may say with justification, if God can quietly do this for one soul, why not for all the others?

This is a good question, and I do not pretend to have the answer. But what I do know is that even in the concentration camps during World War II, there were many who scribbled in the walls, with their fingernails broken and bleeding, words of belief and trust in a Risen Saviour, even (or perhaps especially) in the ruins of a hurting world.

When you think about it, the description in Kings is one that scientists too can embrace, explaining as it does in such real terms the beginnings, avalanche and aftermath of an earthquake, and yet the still, quiet and awesome presence of God when in all the devastation there is that glimmer of hope in one young lad beating all the odds.

Keep supporting those who suffer from natural disasters. Our church has started an appeal in the current crisis and so I am sure will many others. Keep supporting financially. Keep praying. Above all, keep believing, however hard, almost impossible even, at times.

May 2015

Pet Hates

*J*ust in case you thought that clergymen and -women are always good-tempered and 'holier than thou' and never do a bit of raving and ranting at times like everybody else, just share with me, if you will, a few 'pet hates' of mine. And if you like them, I might share a few more next month as well. Then again… it probably won't get me anywhere.

- *Tailgating.* Drivers speeding right up to the back of your car with no consideration for anyone's safety and the need you may have to suddenly brake. The times I have prayed for having one of my old cars back which had the facility for me to open the boot from the inside and let mad drivers through…! Come right in, why don't you?
- *Road humps and sleeping policemen.* How an emergency ambulance going fast (or even one that has to go slow to safeguard the patient) can ever manage these, I'll never know. And what they do to any car suspension and tyre as the humps get worn down and/or the edges sharpen is anyone's guess. I could point the Council to any number of humps within less than a mile from my house where, to protect my car, I now seriously consider putting it in neutral and pushing it across. Dare me!
- *Passwords.* How many do you have? Well, I've lost count! All I know with mine is that somewhere in there is my favourite number, though it's knowing where in the sequence it is! More often than not, I just press 'Forgot password?' and get the chance to pick a new one, and actually doing that on a regular basis – even if you do happen to remember the old one – should increase security, should it not? More often than not I avoid buying anything online that requires a password. It is still just about possible, and you know what? You can still go to the local shop and buy a newspaper without one!

So, there we are! That feels a lot better. Well, you may not, but I do! No wonder Margaret calls me Victor Mildew! As you can see, we are human after all, just in case you wondered.

October 2015

An Advent Prayer for Peace

I find it hard to believe – and I am sure you will too when I tell you – that next month will be my 50th 'Thought' since I arrived on these shores. So that golden anniversary 'Thought' will just have to be a bit special – and how can it not be, seeing that it will be my Christmas message to you all?

However, before that – and in fact quite soon – we shall start our journey through Advent as we prepare for the big event, and rightly so. Advent is when we think about something about to happen, something imminent. As Christians we think about our Lord, coming that first time in all innocence, and about the time when we are promised He will come again. We wonder how it will be then, and the Bible suggests it will be very different and that only God knows the time, the place and the way.

The world was chaotic when Jesus first came, and the world is chaotic today. Often people say that not much has changed over 2,000 years and that, in fact, times now are infinitely more dangerous and hopeless than they were then during the rule of the Roman Empire. Now, they say, the enemy is much more 'obscure', secret, harder to define, the weaponry far more sophisticated, the risk of an all-out war almost too real. And you can see where they are coming from.

Jesus did not mince His words when it came to war. One reading I shall be preaching on, come November 11th this year, is Luke 14 where in verses 31 and 32 we read, "If a king is going to fight another king, first he will sit down and plan. He will decide if he and his 10,000 soldiers can defeat the other king who has 20,000 soldiers. If he can't, then while the other king is still far away, he will send some people to speak to him and ask for peace." I think the crucial words here are "while the other king (or military chief) is still far away", as they ask us to pray and prepare in patience and perseverance. And thank God that even today in the direst of situations, those in authority (though not always agreeing) often determine to meet and talk, knowing that the consequences if they do not could result in disaster.

Let us never stop praying for a peaceful world, and today may our quiet prayers for peace reach to the ends of the universe.

November 2015

Easter Smiles

My Easter message this year is not what perhaps you might expect by way of a scriptural reference to the rising from dead of our Saviour Jesus Christ, however triumphant and assuring that message is for all of us. Rather, I want to share with you the value of something as 'simple' as a smile, as in a world of so much uncertainty and danger, we cannot and should not but smile when we recognise that the victory is already won. I share it with you for two reasons:

1. Jesus on the cross in His dying moments still had time, with a smile, to hand over the apostle John to the loving care of His own mother Mary, and to ask Mary to consider John as her own son too. This is what many of us would have remembered on Mothering Sunday – surely enough to make us smile with gratitude.

2. Jesus died but was risen and He lives for evermore. And here is what I believe we are asked to do in return for that knowledge and privilege, not just at Easter time, but throughout the year:

The Value of a Smile

A smile costs nothing, but means so much. It enriches those who receive it, without making poorer those who give. It takes but a moment, but the memory of it sometimes lasts a lifetime. No one is so rich or mighty that they can get along without it and no one is so poor but would be richer for its benefits. A smile creates happiness in the home, fosters goodwill in business and is the trademark of friendship. It brings rest to the weary, cheer to the discouraged, sunshine to the sad and it is nature's best antidote for trouble. Yet it cannot be bought, begged, borrowed or stolen, for it is something that is of no value to anyone until it is given away. Some people are too tired to give you a smile. Give them one of yours, for nobody needs a smile so much as one who has none left to give.[2]

I cannot remember where or even when I first read these words, but I know it was decades ago. To me they are appropriate to the times we

---

[22] Raoul Follereau; *Le Livre d'Amour* (1920); translated

live in now, and I can but offer them to you this Eastertime. To just slightly paraphrase Strictly Come Dancing, *keep smiling!*

March 2016

The Buzz at Pentecost

*T*wo great events are taking place in Caldicot in the near future. The first event is at Caldicot Castle on May 14th, when two neighbouring Methodist circuits join together within the Castle grounds to celebrate the birthday of the church, Pentecost, as well as the 90th birthday year of HM The Queen. There will be lots of fun and activities, music and singing, craft and entertainment for people of all ages.

The second event is The American Mission Week which starts on May 15th and which will offer us all loads of activities and opportunities made possible by a group of evangelists coming over from the States, and taking place at so many different venues and times throughout our town. The week starts with an open air morning service at the Castle led by the Baptist Church, but that is only the beginning! Publicity with all the details is circulating even as I write this, and my personal thanks must go to Bethany Baptist Church headed by Reverend John Hall who has been busy organizing everything for such a very long time. This is a true Community event with something for everyone, and there is a real buzz about the place.

And talking about a *buzz...* What better time to have all this happening than at Pentecost, when God sent His Spirit to 'speak' and engage with people of all nationalities, languages and backgrounds? And you know what? That first Pentecost was not an isolated incident. God's Spirit continues to appear and reappear to His people and to those who are still searching and, dare I say it, to all who may think they couldn't care less. Whether you are a long-in-the-tooth Christian or just starting out, do join in the church's Pentecost celebrations. It won't cost you a penny but the rewards could be immeasurable.

May 2016

Healing and Wholeness

*I*f you are a regular churchgoer at this time of year, you will find that whatever major denomination you belong to, we are journeying through the Gospel of Luke (my favourite, by the way), and concentrating especially on Jesus going about healing people. Some of those miracles are truly amazing – a word used far too often and in the wrong contexts today, but yes, what Jesus achieved with and for individual people by way of physical healing was amazing, no other word for it. People who had literally died were brought back to life – sometimes by His touch; sometimes by the faith of the bereaved; and sometimes, in the views of bystanders, He would even heal someone they did not really think deserved it. And we marvel when we read these stories.

However, what we need to bear in mind, then as now, is the fact that however many times we may be healed physically, one day we shall die. Together with Income Tax, these are the two things in life we can be sure about: tax and death. For Jesus, death was not the end. So, when He healed, it was for a time and for a purpose, but above all it was to show people the power of God and, most important, in the healing to bring people closer to an understanding of Heaven too, by way of preparing them.

Howard Booth, many decades ago, wrote a couple of books entitled *Healing and Wholeness*, and I think this is right; you cannot have one without the other. Physically and eventually we die, but spiritually (and often through temporary healing) we become more whole as we see the power of God working in and through us. How often we hear people say that it was through their struggle that they gained an inner strength and often saw their faith increased.

I am sorry if my 'Thought' this month is a bit on the 'heavy' side, but it is a subject that we as Christians are asked to consider in our churches this summer, and I can only hope that some of what I have written may be helpful to you if, perhaps physically, you are not at your best right now. Rest assured that Jesus can and will make you feel whole, also in adversity, if only you ask Him.

June 2016

My E-mail Free Zone

*P*eople who ring me, and are patient and caring enough to leave a message on my answerphone if I am not in, are often amused when my recorded message finishes, "Please note that Preben and Margaret take Monday as their day off, and Monday is also a computer free and e-mail free zone." I guess many – when they have stopped giggling – ask themselves, "How can he cope with a whole day without being online?" and, "Why is Monday his day off?"

Well, let us take the last one first, because that's easy: the Church won't let me have Sunday(!), and Saturdays are often occupied with weddings and church fetes and suchlike. So, Monday it is. And Monday is sacrosanct, and the two of us never worry about going away and doing what we want to do for the day, as there are always colleagues with a different day off who will stand in for us.

So do I get withdrawal symptoms without e-mail access for one day a week? No, I do not. And is it back to work with a vengeance on a Tuesday morning with dozens and dozens of mails to sift through? Yes, it is. Although, once all the 'junk' is deleted, it is never all that bad! For me, Monday has become like a holiday, or should I say a Holy Day to look forward to every week throughout the year, and I can only commend it to you if you have not already tried – one day a week to yourself or with your loved one and with no electronic intrusions. Bliss.

August is holiday time. And someone asked me a little while back, "Did Jesus ever go on holiday?" My answer is that we are not told, but we do know that He respected all the Jewish Holy Days, and there are many of those, and we also remember that He liked to take time aside with Mary and Martha and Lazarus, or to go into the mountains to be on His own and to spend time in prayer with God – to reflect and recharge and feel nearer to His Father in the calm and hospitality of a family home or in the beautiful nature all around Him on a mountaintop. And isn't this what holidays and observing Holy Days is all about – a little time away from the usual humdrum of life?

Whatever you are up to this summer, I urge you to find some quality time for yourself (Jesus did) and even if it means unplugging the computer for just one day (something that Jesus never had to worry about 2,000 years ago, but which can be a real problem in our day and time). God bless you – and relax!

Ability, Not Disability

The Paralympics have not long finished in Rio, at the time of writing, and if you are anything like Margaret and me, you will have been full of admiration at what you saw: the dedication of those taking part, and all of them without every limb and faculty many of us take so for granted. Just as we could not fail to be impressed with the Olympics, there was something quite special about what we witnessed over the last few weeks on our screens, and thank God for Channel 4 for providing such extensive and excellent coverage.

Disability? Don't you believe it. We saw nothing short of various abilities before us that most able-bodied people could not even dream of attempting – me least of all, who am not a sporty person by any stretch of the imagination. Years of toil, patience, sweat, pain and tears paid off right there in front of our eyes, and we stood back at times in disbelief.

I have mentioned before that Margaret and I are part of a team who once a month lead our PROSPECTS group at church, for and with people with learning disabilities, and for some this can mean physical as well as psychological problems. Once again it is *ability* we see expressed in craft, signing, praying, singing, drama and generally joining together and pooling all our resources. For our friends it is not a question of anything 'missing', it is a matter of making the most of everything they and we have been gifted with together, each one of us. It is no surprise that once a year PROSPECTS recommend and provide service details for what is known as Ability Sunday; note again, *ability* not *disability*.

As Christians we read in the Bible and we believe that each one of us is created in the image of God, and that means being shaped into someone beautiful and important – each a masterpiece shaped by the Master's hand. The recent couple of weeks in Rio brought this home and could leave no doubt in anyone's mind that God loves us and equips us for great things, whoever we are and whatever our circumstances. God bless you.

September 2016

Remembrance Sunday

*R*emembrance Sunday should never be forgotten. Nor should we ever forget these words, "They shall not grow old, as we that are left grow old: age shall not weary them, nor the years condemn. At the going down of the sun and in the morning, we will remember them." They appear in the middle of the poem *For the Fallen*, written by Laurence Binyon in 1914 at the start of the First World War. This was two years before the Battle of the Somme in 1916, the centenary of which we remember this year – one of the bloodiest battles in history and with an incredible loss of life.

For the Fallen begins with these words: "With proud thanksgiving, a mother for her children, England mourns for her dead across the sea. Flesh of her flesh they were, spirit of her spirit, fallen in the cause of the free." The two keywords are 'proud thanksgiving', and no doubt these are feelings and sentiments shared by people throughout the world also today when in many ways war is very different and more 'secretive' compared to what it used to be. Today we have to face cyberwars, terrorist atrocities, secret and deadly deals being brokered which, perhaps thankfully, we know little or nothing about. However, the sacrifices made by those who serve the cause and the agonies suffered by those who mourn their dead are just the same, unchanged, undiminished, indeed unbearable.

Being the current chaplain for Caldicot British Legion, you will not be surprised to hear me say that we must never forget Remembrance Sunday, but always continue to remember and honour those who gave – and continue to give – their lives that we may live. You do not have to be a Christian to make that promise, although of course as Christians we have Jesus as our example of the ultimate sacrifice, yet in that, promising each one of us new life for evermore. Rarely in history has that assurance and truth been more important to hear and to share.

For the Fallen ends with these words: "As the stars that shall be bright when we are dust, moving in marches upon the heavenly plain; as the stars that are starry in the time of our darkness, to the end, to the end, they remain" – "they" being 'the fallen', now as then, without whom you and I just would not be.

November 2016

Peace on Earth at Christmas

The ancient Chinese philosopher and writer Lao Tzu (570-490 BC) wrote the following: "If there is to be peace in the world, there must be peace in the nations. If there is to be peace in the nations, there must be peace in the cities. If there is to be peace in the cities, there must be peace between neighbours. If there is to be peace between neighbours, there must be peace in the home. If there is to be peace in the home, there must be peace in the heart."

I would like to focus on the subject of Peace for a few months, as surely this is what we all pray about and strive for, and try to determine how it can be achieved. After all, does not the popular song give us this challenge: "Let there be peace on earth, and let it begin with me"?

May we never underestimate the power and ability we each have to achieve great things through small beginnings, and how so often the first step is by setting our mind firmly on something. So why not make that 'something' Peace in the year ahead.

Jesus came with a message of Peace into a world of war and hatred and occupation, just like it is today. He spoke God's message without faltering, even to death, and today two billion people round the world continue to proclaim the Word, often by taking great risks in areas of persecution, now as then. Little has changed, but that also includes the human spirit and the power of God through us, by grace and perseverance enabling us to do great things, individually and corporately.

So, my Christmas message this year is Peace in all its promise, variety, and yes, difficulty in achieving. Let me begin to draw to a close by quoting Mother Theresa (1910-1997) who said this: "If we have no peace, it is because we have forgotten that we belong to each other."

For now, may the Prince of Peace go with you this Christmastime and into the New Year.

December 2016

Love in the New Year

Continuing the theme of Peace, how about these quotes by two famous people, though with many years between them: "When the power of love overcomes the love of power, the world will know peace" (Jimi Hendrix) and "We look forward to the time when the Power of Love will replace the Love of Power. Then will our world know the blessings of peace." (William Gladstone).

It seems to me that both gentlemen from very different eras touch on something really significant, not least in this time of uncertainty and fear relating to animosity and warmongering between the world's most powerful nations. What a start to the New Year this is, with talk of cyberspace wars which, for a good many of us, is a subject we just cannot begin to understand.

Both Jimi Hendrix and William Gladstone come to the same conclusion, that without good (love) overcoming bad (power), and indeed without love *replacing* power, nothing will change. Perhaps the time has come for each one of us to shout out loud, "Enough is enough!" and to start positively working towards something better, something lasting.

For churchgoers this quest is pursued as fellow believers meet week by week, often day by day, to support and strengthen one another in Bible study and in prayer. For those not associated with church, the quest can still be real and significant, though sometimes it may feel lonely without the backing and support that the church family can offer. As Reverend Dr Martin Luther King, Jr. put it so succinctly, "When we let freedom ring, when we let it ring from every village and every hamlet, from every state and every city, we will be able to speed up that day when all of God's children, black and white, Jews and Gentiles, Protestants and Catholics, will be able to join hands and sing in the words of the old Negro spiritual, 'Free at last! Free at last! Thank God Almighty, we are free at last!'"

May God bless you all as we watch a world in turmoil, and perhaps especially the power struggles between the world's mightiest nations, but may we never fail in standing united at every opportunity and pray for world peace and respect and understanding between all people everywhere.

The Personal Touch

*I*t's time for a moan. Oh no, not again, I can hear from those who know me well, but so be it. And come on, we haven't had a real one for a very long time in this column!

This may come as a surprise to some, but I actually enjoy going into my local bank, especially when I have something to deposit, but equally to have a human being to talk to if things need sorting. I always find the staff behind the tills helpful and courteous and with time for you, and yes, these are things I really appreciate.

Imagine my terror, therefore, when this morning I was handed a slip to say that in a little over a month's time my bank will only be open on three weekdays and shut on two, but that "online banking is available 24 hours". Yes, I am sure it is, but as a principle I don't do online banking and I am not about to start now. That's all, full stop. When I go to my bank, I go to get a good service, see a friendly face, exchange a few kind remarks, and hand over or take out my hard-earned money with the willing assistance of a professional human being always happy to help.

I do sometimes wonder how many members of staff – not to mention customers – are consulted before decisions to severely limit opening times or close branches are taken. I cannot remember ever having been asked my opinion, can you?

Let's get back to being personal in this world today. Let's not forget the value and spring to the step a kindly word and a helpful act can give; the difference, in fact, this can be to many people's lives, including but not exclusively the elderly, the lonely and those who feel technologically oppressed – and I think we are many in today's world. I get a little tired of pressing buttons on a keyboard all the time to get anywhere and to get things moving. The personal approach has to be the better one.

So there we have it, my rant for the month. Back to normal next time, perhaps – whatever is normal... Thank you for listening, and I just hope I have spoken for some in our community this month.

March 2017

The Evidence for Easter

I came across a fascinating article by Matt Perman entitled 'Historical Evidence for the Resurrection', and what better Easter message than to share some of his thoughts with you this month?

- The Empty Tomb accounts in the Gospels, albeit with slight variations in the narrative, are remarkable in being recorded so relatively soon after they happened, and in the evident urgency of getting the good news spread by those who had heard of, and some even witnessed, the events for themselves.
- Jesus' tomb was never venerated as a shrine. It was a first century custom to set up a shrine at the site of a holy man's bones. There were at least 50 such shrines in Jesus' day. There being no such shrine for Jesus indicates that His bones weren't there, that He was not there!
- When Jesus appeared several times after His Resurrection, He was found eating and drinking with His disciples, and He invited them to touch Him. Jesus was able to appear, disappear and reappear at God's will, literally, but always in a shape and form already known to those who knew and loved Him.

There are many more pieces of evidence one could list, but suffice it to say here and now that perhaps the strongest evidence for the Resurrection is the existence of the Christian church and the testimony of believers to this day expressing their trust in Jesus. We do so as we recognise that He is the only religious leader who was risen from the dead. No other world religion can lay claim to this. Christianity is the only religion that believes Jesus to be both God and man, i.e. totally divine yet at the same time wholly human. All religions agree He was a good man, a teacher and a prophet, but only Christianity, thanks to the evidence, acknowledges Him as the Son of God.

Mark's Gospel, believed to be the earliest of the four, was written about AD 50 or about 15 years after the events – far too soon to become history or legend, but early enough to carry eyewitness reports and give hope and assurance to this day for all believers, as well as for those still searching.

April 2017

The Good Shepherd

We have just finished Christian Aid week, which this year ran from May 14th through to the 20th. Many people, as always, supported this worthwhile cause in every way they could, as rarely in human history has the need been greater amongst God's people, on the African continent and in many other parts of the world too.

In our churches we have just celebrated the period of the year when we concentrate on Jesus the Good Shepherd, and I thought this month we could have a quick look at sheep and shepherds in biblical times 2,000 years ago. At the time of Christ, the shepherd's job was a dirty and dangerous one, as often all the shepherd would have to fight off lions and other wild animals with was his staff with a crook. At night, he would put the flock in a makeshift pen that had only one way in and out. The shepherd would open the door to the pen, call the sheep by name, and they would come in and settle safely for the night. Then the shepherd, once the flock was safely gathered in, would lie down at the gate to the pen, to give his life if necessary to protect his flock.

The Gospels have several references to Jesus the Good Shepherd, and of course we all know and love the hymn based on Psalm 23 which starts, "The Lord's my Shepherd; I'll not want." The word 'want' on this occasion covers a multitude of reassurances, as Jesus tells us not to *worry*, not to *fear*, not to *wander*, but to know the security and assurance only He can give us in troubled times, in His pen.

I may well have mentioned this before, but in the Holy Land, to this day, the shepherd walks ahead of his flock, not behind them as in most other countries, trusting them to follow him, to recognise and obey his voice and listen to his commands. We may sometimes find it more difficult today to 'hear' Jesus in the noise and confusion and warmongering of everyday life, but when you think about it, who else can we picture literally laying down his life for each one of us, by day and by night, at every moment we are awake and when we are asleep?

May 2017

Summer Opportunities

I hope you are enjoying the hot spells we experience occasionally, although many people I speak to much prefer the cooler temperatures and find it very hard to cope with warm and humid nights when, after all, you need your beauty sleep ready to face the new day.

Summer is traditionally supposed to be a little quieter than other times of the year, but you would not believe that in the Andersen household. Although many regular church events are about to take a well-deserved break until September, there is still much to do, many opportunities to grasp and, if possible, run with, and always of course people in need, in hospital, at home, and those you meet who have lost a loved one and where the necessary funeral arrangements have to be made. Such duties never stop, nor should they, come sun, come rain, come anything in between.

As many of you will know, I am the current chaplain for the Caldicot British Legion and that is a great privilege. God willing, I am now also about to become chaplain for the Caldicot Air Cadets. It just goes to show how desperate people can get, doesn't it? No, in all seriousness, I look forward to it very much, to interact with, talk and listen to the Cadets, and to the sterling volunteers who do so much good work for them and with them.

I believe life in all its variety is about grasping the nettle and tackling the opportunities God sends our way, as we are able and willing. My Margaret keeps reminding me that hard work never killed anyone, and as my late Dad used to say exactly the same thing, albeit in Danish, I just have to believe it, don't I? For me, the work I feel God calling me to do, even on a hot day, is the best of all and the most worthwhile, and those calls can come at any time and often unexpectedly, literally out of the blue. As did the e-mail from the Air Cadets.

Have a great summer, wherever it takes you, on well-deserved breaks or into ventures unknown. And know God by your side in every step you take.

July 2017

Seventy

Believe it or not, but this is my 70th monthly 'Thought' in the Free Press. And that made me think about the significance of the numbers seven, and indeed 70, in the Bible. Did you know, for example, that the number seven appears in the Bible more than 700 times? Of course, not every instance of the number seven in the Bible carries a deeper significance, but it is true to say that often it seems that seven communicates the meaning of divine completeness, perfection and wholeness.

In the first book of the Bible, Genesis, God spends six days working hard on creating the heavens and the earth, and on the seventh day He rests. And in last book of the Bible, Revelation, we find reference to seven letters to seven churches, seven spirits before the throne of God, seven golden lampstands, seven stars in Jesus' right hand, seven angels with seven trumpets, and I could go on. The number 70 comes in when Simon Peter asks Jesus how many times he is expected to forgive his brother and sister, and Jesus replies, "I tell you, not seven times, but seventy times seven," (Matthew 18:22) meaning an infinitely large number, and that each and every one of us should be generous and tireless in forgiving one another.

I guess you too have your favourite number? As it happens, I do like seven, although my absolute favourite is three. Why? I wish I knew, and that I could give some biblical reason for it, such as the Trinity perhaps (Father, Son and Holy Spirit), but no, my heart for the number three goes back to long before I became a Christian. However, once you pick your favourite number, don't you find that they easily take on a real significance for you, and you tend to use them in passwords and such like as they are easily remembered?

Whatever your favourite number, treasure it, but do not use it in all your passwords! And remember that numbers in the Bible were often simply translated by the words 'many' or 'several' instead. One number we can all agree on of course is this: Jesus is and always will be our Number One. God bless you.

August 2017

Making a Difference

"There's a time for everything and a season for every activity under heaven: a time to be born and a time to die, a time to plant and a time to uproot, a time to kill and a time to heal, a time to tear down and a time to build, a time to weep and a time to laugh, a time to mourn and a time to dance, ... a time to tear and a time to mend, a time to be silent and a time to speak, a time to love and a time to hate, a time for war and a time for peace." (Ecclesiastes 3:1-4,7-8)

This is a well-known excerpt from an Old Testament book, generally believed to have been written by King Solomon and probably dating back to about 950 BC. Some critics detect in these verses a grumpy old man looking at the world at large with a very resigned frame of mind and kind of saying, "What will be will be, and there's nothing I can do about it, so I may as well go with it. Such is the world, a mixture of good and bad."

Of course, for some this may well be one solution in such an unstable world, then as now: to just go with it. Yet for many of us there is a need and a desire to continue to put our trust in God and pray for a better and more peaceful future, until the day comes when – in the words of a popular hymn – "at the name of Jesus every knee shall bow, every tongue confess Him King of Glory now". Not at some point in the future – but King of Glory *now*.

It is all too easy sometimes to simply continue on the merry-go-round without trusting in something – Someone – better, and to think that we can make no difference in helping to make the world a better place. If everyone thinks like that then certainly it won't be. So, let us persevere, even in adversity, and march forward in trust and confidence, and not be grumpy old people never expecting anything to change for the better. This is still a beautiful world inhabited for the most part by good people, and we should never forget that.

October 2017

The Joy of Travelling

Margaret and I have just returned from our first ever visit to Eire. Crossing and returning on the ferry, from Fishguard and Rosslaire respectively, and the smoothest of crossings both ways (contrary to what many 'kind' people had told us to expect), the holiday came off to a calm start as well as a smooth end. And the bits in between were not bad either.

What a beautiful country, and how charming and welcoming the Irish people! Nothing was too much trouble, and "no worries" seemed to be the stock answer to most things. The roads were mainly quiet, the landscape varied and beautiful, and the whole atmosphere relaxing and comforting, which of course is what you pray for on holiday. We marvelled at the crystal factory and Viking museum in Waterford (where, being Danish, I could say hello to my forefathers!), the Titanic experience in Cobh, the blarney stone at the top of the castle, and visits to Tipperary (a long, long way away!) and Cork, to mention but a few attractions; not forgetting the beautiful cathedrals and churches we were able to fit in.

All this has made me think how Paul and his missionaries in the early church must have enjoyed travelling too, making converts in the process, enjoying God's beautiful creation, and marvelling at all that is good and true and lasting, but which often – and sadly – we take so for granted.

Ours may have been only a six-day 'hop', but we have returned with lots of happy memories, so if there are any Irish people out there reading this, thank you for keeping your countryside so beautiful and maintaining such a spirit of welcome and faithfulness for your visitors to enjoy. It has meant a lot to us both.

November 2017

Advent – Preparing

*A*dvent. The time of preparing – but for what? To get the best deals on Black Friday or, if you missed that, in many places spilling over into Grey Saturday, Mauve Sunday and Blue Monday. Enormous discounts on offer – which always make me wonder, if goods really can be sold that cheap, why can't we buy them at the same price every day of every year? It would make life a whole lot easier…

Advent. Preparing – and for Christians a time when we remember the first Christmas, the birth of Jesus, and at the same time look forward to His coming again as promised in the Bible. For Margaret and me, this time of preparation has taken many forms already, from being able to attend the Festival of Remembrance at Royal Albert Hall (courtesy of the British Legion), to witnessing the switching on the lights in our town, to preparing for the Christmas market this coming Saturday, to getting down to thinking about the numerous services about to happen in our churches. And this seriously begins tonight with our annual Light Up A Life service by St David's Hospice Care, which is always a moving and heart-warming experience.

Losing a loved one is always hard, but losing one in the lead-up to Christmas can be almost impossible to cope with. At a Light Up A Life service like-minded people come together to find but the smallest flicker of hope and warmth and love; and those who mourn can know that they are not on their own, and hopefully, prayerfully find just that small flicker of perseverance and ability to come to terms with it and move on.

Advent. Preparing. This is not, or should not be, a commercial thing. It should be an opportunity for us all to put the Christ child back into Christmas. I do not like the abbreviation 'Xmas'. It takes away Christ, although, in view of what I have just written, it may also remind some of the cross (the 'X') on which He died and the pain of which many will feel very deeply this Christmastime.

May the peace of Christmas and the promise of a good and prosperous New Year be real to each and every one of you, in Jesus' name.

December 2017

Jesus in the Snow

*R*ecently, we have had a lot of snow, which has brought to my memory the story of the picture known as 'Jesus in the snow'. A Chinese photographer, so the story goes, was in a bad place spiritually, really struggling. He longed to know Jesus as his master and friend and, as he walked along, said to himself, "Lord, if only I could see your face, I would believe." Instantly a voice spoke to his heart, saying, "Take a picture. Take a picture. Go on. Do it now." Looking round, he did not immediately see anything to take a picture of, but still felt compelled to take one. So he aimed the lens at some melting snow with the black earth showing through it, got the film developed, and from the black and white areas of the snow scene, a face seemed to look at him, full of tenderness and love – the face of Christ? He believed so, and as a result he became a Christian.

Look at the picture above. Can you see Jesus in it? Some can; others try hard and then have to give up. Still others give it a break, then come back later, try again, and see it – see Jesus. How about you? Will you get it in one, or two, or three, if at all?

The good news is that it is no disaster if you don't see it, for truly 'seeing' Jesus, sensing His presence, allowing Him into your heart, all start from a desire to know Him, and then trusting in God who by His grace gives us the faith to believe in and to feel His love. No picture can do all this, only a searching mind and a believing and welcoming heart.

Free Press, March 2018

Easter Blockbusters

*D*id you manage to see at least one biblical blockbuster over Easter? I admit, they are never all that easy to find, especially on terrestrial television, but Margaret and I did appreciate The Robe that showed on Good Friday afternoon. And then, two days running, and leading up to Easter Day, Sky Classics showed three blockbusters, namely Spartacus, The Bible and The Ten Commandments. I have them recorded, but as they are at least three hours long – each – it's a matter of finding the time.

We did laugh, though, as one of them, because it is so long, had 'Intermission' halfway through (as they did in the cinemas in years gone by), but it was peculiar on the telly to have ten minutes with just the intermission sign (until I realised that I could, of course, fast forward it a bit!) No hope…

Also, in the cinemas, we now have Mary Magdalene. There have been mixed reviews (as always when we have a Christian movie), but although I admit there is quite a bit of poetic and biblical licence in it, no one can take the piety away from it, and it was a good and gentle and loving film with not a swear word to be heard.

Churches Together, for whom I am the current Chairman, are toying with the idea of a quarterly movie night at my church, where we can watch a religious film and enjoy the obligatory popcorn and can of coke at the same time! Nothing is finalised yet, and no doubt it will need to go before various councils first for approval – but why not? We have the screen, the laptop and the projector – not to mention Dominos right opposite us (so, pizza as well as popcorn?) I can see great things happening.

All this leads me to conclude that God's Not Dead – the title of yet another great film by the way – and that we should take every opportunity to enjoy and encourage films that are as loved today as they were when many of them were first produced 60 or 70 years ago, with intermission and all. Happy viewing; keep searching!

April 2018

Surprising Bible Facts

*T*his month I have dipped into the internet – as one does – to find a number of interesting Bible facts and figures for you, some of which you may well know, while others might surprise you (as they did me). No wonder the Bible – or God's Living Word – is the book found on most bookshelves and in the most languages throughout the world. Just have a look at this:

- There are over 7,000 languages and dialects in today's world and the Bible is available (wholly or partly) in 2,500 of them. This means, of course, that 4,500 languages still wait for even one book of the Bible to be translated.
- The Bible Society estimates that close to six billion Bibles have been printed over the last couple of hundred years alone. Considering that the total world population today is estimated at 7.6 billion people, that's not bad, I think. In fact, it is believed that about 50 Bibles are sold every minute.
- "Do not be afraid" occurs 365 times in the Bible – and isn't that comforting, to know that for every day of the year we can have that assurance and comfort for free and by the grace of God?

If ever you wanted to help support a charity in a novel way and felt inclined to sit and read the whole Bible from cover to cover out loud in front of your congregation at church, it would likely take you about 70 hours to do so – longer, of course, if you need to have the occasional coffee break!

Finally this, which I can quite understand, having worked as a translator and interpreter before I was called to the ministry: the whole process of producing a translation of the Bible is slow, difficult and lengthy, although thanks to computer-aided programmes available today, there is now a reduction in the time involved. This can only be good and should be welcomed, and it is also good that, for all its pitfalls, the internet does contain much excellent biblical information just by a bit of googling and the press of a button. Happy surfing!

July 2018

Serenity

The American theologian Reinhold Niebuhr wrote what has become known as the Serenity Prayer in 1934, and both Margaret and I found it interesting to hear it said by one of the main characters in the fourth and final series of the Danish and Swedish crime series The Bridge recently. In fact, Margaret said to me, "I used to have this one written down in front of me somewhere."

For those of you who find yourselves in a similar position and would like to be reminded of the words, here they are: "God, grant me the serenity to accept the things I cannot change, courage to change the things I can, and wisdom to know the difference."

Simple as that, except of course it is rarely quite that simple.

The prayer was originally used by Niebuhr in his sermons and house groups, but later it was adopted by Alcoholics Anonymous and other community organisations to help people in their personal struggles.

My 'Thought' this month is brief. Margaret and I have not long been back from Denmark where we attended the service for, and in my case presented the Tribute to, my dear Mother at her funeral. We have all experienced the loss of a loved one and know how difficult it can be to come to terms, and how 'unreal' the days, weeks and months that follow may seem. In my case, I was blessed with Mum who was always thankful, never complained, was well looked after when she needed it most, much loved, and who at the end was not at all frightened but fully prepared to meet her Maker after a good and a long life well lived.

May the words of Niebuhr's prayer serve to guide each one of us through difficult times, knowing that by asking God to grant us His help, we need not worry as we are enabled to carry on.

August 2018

10,000 Miles Without a Car

Margaret and I were discussing only the other day how many miles we must have spent driving to Denmark and back since September 2014 when the Harwich to Esbjerg ferry route stopped after 140 years of service. I estimate that with one trip in 2014, and two trips each year between 2015 and 2018, and with just under 800 miles to travel each way each time, we are looking at something like 14,400 miles (and that is not counting the mileage clocked up – though admittedly a lot less each time – when the more direct ferry link did exist and we still journeyed to and fro every year for 40 years). It makes the mind boggle.

Imagine my surprise, therefore, when I read somewhere that the apostle Paul managed around 10,000 miles over 30 years on his many missionary journeys, to places as widespread as Ephesus, Philippi, Corinth and Athens, to mention but a few – not forgetting Malta where he was shipwrecked! Just think for a moment how restricted he was compared to now with means of transport, how longer the ships would have taken and how much walking would have been involved to get from port to port.

You know, I feel almost ashamed at my own calculations in comparison! My destination was always the same, the route did not change, there were no diversions, the people we met and whose company we enjoyed so much over the years (Mother's especially) were much the same, and I am afraid I did not do much, if any, evangelising on my travels (I was enjoying myself too much).

So, yes, Paul deserves our respect. His journeys involved arrest and torture, many imprisonments, and still he managed to spread the gospel, the Good News, to all the known world without all the modern commodities, including the high speed cars we have at hand today. In AD 313 Christianity was formally and universally accepted by Emperor Constantine and only ten years later it had become the official religion of the Roman Empire. The rest, as they say, is history.

October 2018

World War I – Centenary

This year, as I write, marks the 100th anniversary of the end of World War I, and as chaplain for Caldicot British Legion I am grateful to those who show support and determination to remember and give thanks indeed for all those lives lost that we today may live. I am planning to preach at St Mary's in Caldicot on November 11th and never have I felt more honoured and more determined to include the thoughts and prayers, not only of those who fought (or knew people who did), but also of the very many young people here in our community so determined to ensure we never forget.

Did you know that a total of 16 million lives were lost over four years in the First World War alone as 65 million people from 32 countries were drawn into the conflict? And did you know that the one book that was read and cherished and carried everywhere, above all into combat, by people on all sides was the Bible? It is believed that more than nine million Bibles in 80 languages were translated, printed and sent to members of the Armed forces and to prisoners of war on all sides.

One soldier who survived the war told his family on his return, "I would definitely have been killed were it not for this Bible," and he showed them the shrapnel-damaged Bible which he had held so close to his chest on one particularly ferocious day with bullets flying everywhere. This man was an agnostic – someone who searched for the meaning of life and death but was not sure how and where to find it – but he became a regular churchgoer after the war. His Bible, damaged as it was, stayed close to his heart for the rest of his life, but even more important, from its pages he came to know the living Christ.

World War I should have been the war to end them all, but of course it wasn't. Wars still rage today. Thank God, therefore, that in His living Word, the Bible, we have His Son Jesus to give us hope and comfort, today as ever. God bless you.

November 2018

The Christmas Message

Chances are that my Christmas 'Thought' will be in the Free Press on December 12th, which will be the day after an important 24 hours in Parliament, for the UK, the EU, the world, not to mention each and every one of us as individuals. Ministers will debate whether to have a second referendum to determine whether Brexit will still go ahead.

Compare Brexit to the coming of our Lord Jesus in Bethlehem as a babe on what we celebrate now as the first Christmas. No question, no vote, no debating about that one. In fact, no one but God had any control over what happened when He sent Jesus into an occupied nation inhabited by people many of whom were frightened, disillusioned, fearing for their lives, lonely, desolate.

In some ways nothing much seems to have changed in the secular world since then, yet everything changed forever when God came to earth in the person of Jesus. He came to give hope to the hopeless and extend God's love to all who felt unloved and ignored. Each day somewhere in the world new people continue to come to know Him through the Bible, in church, and from personal testimonies by Christians courageous enough to want to share their good news with others.

You know, I almost died the other day when Margaret and I visited a normal card shop in a high street and found a whole section with the heading 'Christian Christmas Cards'. And it wasn't just one or two cards either, it was row after row of them. How wonderful was that! And how rare an experience too in this day and time. In fact, I haven't found one since...

The Christmas message is one of love, hope and trust in the belief that even in the most difficult of circumstances God is with us. So whatever politicians decide for our future, may this at least be our comfort and encouragement: that God is alive and well.

Merry Christmas and happy New Year!

December 2018

New Year's Revolutions

I wonder how many of us made a New Year's resolution this year. And if we did, how long are we going to be able to keep it for? Maybe one reason why such resolutions are not as popular as perhaps they used to be, lies in the fact that they weren't always realistic or we had no clear plan about how to achieve them. Sometimes a New Year's resolution can seem little more than a wish list, a series of things we'd like to change about our lives, but not much more than that. They can always become very self-centred though; as Christians I believe we should always try to aim higher and ask ourselves, "Is it God's will I am trying to pursue here rather than my own somewhat selfish desire?"

Our daughter Heidi as a teenager never operated with New Year *resolutions* – she called them *revolutions* instead! And when you think about it, there's something to be said for that. If we are going to make them, let's promise to do something really earth-shattering and, yes, revolutionary for God. Why not?

In Jesus' time New Year, as now, was often marked with much noise, including blasts on the trumpets in the temple courts. We don't hear much if anything about fireworks in the Bible though and certainly Madness was not on the scene then, although I have to say I really enjoyed them at Westminster Central Hall on New Year's Eve! Then, as now, New Year was a time for celebration, reminiscing, planning, and for being families and friends together, hoping to do better, trying just that little bit harder.

So, do I have a 'New Year revolution' for this year? In all honesty, not one that springs clearly to mind, though I do pray for a desire and ability to try and achieve an even closer walk with God, in my preparation for worship, through Bible study and by speaking and sharing my love for Him more with the people I engage with and come across. So, no pressure, Andersen!

January 2019

Valentine's Day

*I*t has to be all about love this month, doesn't it, with Valentine's Day? And of course, when we think about the Italian Saint Valentine, who became the patron saint of lovers – and indeed of the Welsh Valentine, Saint Dwynwen, whose saint's day is January 25th every year – it is no doubt a particular kind of physical love we think about first. This is OK as long as we don't stop there but try to move on to an even more exciting and fulfilling kind of love – yes, the one that Jesus gives us.

Jesus' love is not limited to January 25th or February 14th every year; in fact, it is for every moment of every day of every year, and it is freely available to everyone too, simply for the asking. It is that ultimate love that the Greeks call *agape*, and which translates 'love feast' or 'a feast of love'.

Agape is also how we refer to Holy Communion when in churches we come to the Lord's table and share in the bread and the wine, remembering His sacrifice for us on the cross. *Agape* can be described as that all-encompassing and everywhere-present feeling of warmth, compassion and understanding that only God can give in our most difficult circumstances. *Agape*, 'Jesus love', has little if anything to do with that other kind of love that also makes the world go round and which we associate with Valentine, but everything to do with that most sincere and freely given love whereby Jesus gave His life in forgiveness of our sins. There can be no greater sacrifice and no greater gift.

So, yes, by all means let us celebrate Saint Valentine and Saint Dwynwen, and let us spoil one another and express our love in so many wonderful ways – as long as we never forget that *agape* love which is in our breathing and thinking and in our walk with God every moment of every day.

February 2019

Ikigai at Lent

*H*ave you ever heard about *Ikigai?* Well, I hadn't until I attended a three-day course in Hertfordshire recently where the concept was explained to clergy like me who (let's face it) are getting ever closer to retiring gracefully. Not just yet, mind – still some time to go, thankfully.

Ikigai is a Japanese concept that has to do with finding your unique self, your singular talent, your passion in life, and it is based on these Ten Rules, so are you ready?

1. Stay active and don't retire from everything.
2. Take it slow.
3. Eat a little less than your hunger actually demands.
4. Surround yourself with good friends.
5. Exercise – just a bit of gentle daily maintenance will do.
6. Smile.
7. Reconnect with nature.
8. Give thanks.
9. Live in the moment.
10. Find your *Ikigai*, your passion, your unique talent.

Sounds easy when written down like this, doesn't it? But I know I should struggle with (3) and (5) for starters! There's honesty for you.

In future 'Thoughts' I plan to look at just some of these in greater detail, but for now may we remember that we are in the season of Lent leading us eventually to the high point of the Christian year which is Easter Day. And may we also remember that Jesus, during Lent, was tempted and tested in the desert, often lonely, sad and frustrated – wouldn't you be? – yet with His eyes set purposely and never wavering on the road ahead; being Himself prepared, as well as able to prepare others, to follow, to see and, yes, to realise their uniqueness by His guidance and example. Living the moment yet always looking ahead!

There's a lot to take in during Lent and this is why in so many churches Lent courses are taking place to stimulate us all in our thinking and helping us become the best that we can be.

March 2019

Mary's Easter Hope

*L*ive in the moment. This was one of the ten recommendations I listed last month and I hope that what I am going to share with you now may serve to help us do more of that – live in and be thankful for each new day.

Holidays are always good times for contemplation and taking stock, and for Margaret and me it was a privilege and pleasure to be able to worship in Malta on Mothering Sunday at St Andrew's church in Valetta, which is described as a Union of Church of Scotland and the Methodist Church. One hymn in particular spoke to us both in the service, and the last two verses helped us realise the true significance of Easter. I share them with you as my Easter message this year. The hymn is called 'Mary, Joyful Mother', written by Gillian Collins, but as you will read in just a moment, and as Lent has reminded us as we now culminate with Easter, not everything in the garden was rosy nor was every step Jesus took an easy one, for Him or for His mother. And yet, as we come to the pinnacle of the Christian year and look back as well as looking forward, we realise that Mary's feelings are our feelings too at times when life is difficult and hurtful, hopeless even.

The Easter hope is precisely that there is always Hope, for all of us, and assurance too. So, please can I ask you to take a moment to read the two verses with which I finish this 'Thought' and ponder them this Easter?

> *Mary, watching sadly by the cruel cross,*
> *Who can know your thoughts now, grieving in your loss?*
> *Was it all for this, then? All your years of care?*
> *He cries, "It is finished!" You weep with despair.*
>
> *Mary, new disciple, in the upper room,*
> *Waiting, watching, praying – Spirit's coming soon.*
> *Mother of the Christ-child, suffering, faithful, true,*
> *We have now a Saviour. God be praised for you!*

April 2019

Pentecost – Breaking Down Barriers

God dag; buenos dias; guten tag; bonjour; mahalo; ohayo gozaimasu; dobri ranok; shalom; good day! Danish, Spanish, German, French, Hawaiian, Japanese, Ukrainian, Hebrew and English – hello, everybody! So many languages yet the same meaning. Just like that first Pentecost two thousand or so years ago when God sent His Spirit to all those waiting in Jerusalem and ensuring that the world would never be the same again.

Pentecost Sunday is also known as the birthday of the church, when the Spirit came to give new life and hope and assurance. It follows so soon after Ascension Sunday when we remember how Jesus left us for a while but assures us that (1) He will return and (2) while we wait, God's Spirit is with us, within us and above us too.

The Coming of the Spirit was the common denominator in a way that enabled all peoples to understand one another, if not always by their language alone then certainly by freeing their spiritual dimension and wanting to praise the Living God. They did then, and billions of people throughout the world continue to do so today.

The 19th century poet William Blake wrote a poem entitled 'Pentecost'. It is brief but profound and I want to share it with you here. "Unless the eye catch fire the God will not be seen. Unless the ear catch fire the God will not be heard. Unless the tongue catch fire the God will not be named. Unless the heart catch fire the God will not be loved. Unless the mind catch fire the God will not be known."

The book of Acts tells what happens at Pentecost in a very dramatic way and in a form which can only be an eye witness report. Read it for yourselves in Acts 2:1-21 and rejoice, in whichever language you are comfortable.

June 2019

Air Cadets

As I am writing this tonight I have just finished preparing for my Padre's Hour at the Air Cadets Squadron where I attend roughly once every four to five weeks. Sometimes the young Cadets and I share religious matters, but more often we talk about what goes on in the world generally and what makes the young folk 'tick' today. It is always inspiring and interesting and I always leave the group feeling on a high.

Or should I say, I *did* until their training officer had the brilliant idea a few months back that he thought their chaplain should have a go at their flight simulator! Without going into too much detail about it, I do wonder how many of my juniors ever managed to crash the plane four times on the runway even before take-off... Yes, I guess that must be some record and I can only thank my Lord that my driving a car seems to be slightly better than that!

The flight simulator apart, the enjoyment I get from Padre's Hour is beyond words. The interaction with the young people and their leaders is second to none. The questions I am often asked, the Christian music (like Graham Kendrick) I am permitted to play for them, the Bible readings we share too, are all such opportunities. I thank God every day for the privilege of being helped by them all to feel young again.

So there we are. Hardly a word about Jesus or religion this month. Worry not, that won't last, for I really believe He is the 'driving force' in all our lives, on a good day and on days when things are more difficult. Which reminds me, the Squadron calls and on my walk there I will just have to try and think of some excuse not to get anywhere near that flight simulator. Any suggestions?

July 2019

Also by Preben Andersen

Living Through Lockdown
Publisher: Onwards and Upwards
ISBN: 978-1-78815-582-3

From the first news of the Covid-19 outbreak in the UK, to the hope arising from a vaccination programme being put into place, Rev. Preben Andersen has written poetry to keep a record of our shared 2020 pandemic experiences in the UK. His poems cover the politics and the scramble to understand the science, but also the daily experiences and sacrifices we have all had to make, and the challenges for frontline workers, school children, separated families and others. Behind it all, Preben recognises a God who is still on the throne, and working in our lives even as our experience of church has changed.

Available from all good bookshops and from the publisher:
www.onwardsandupwards.org